AEGIS

AEGIS

SELECTED POEMS 1970~1980

CID CORMAN

STATION HILL

Published by Station Hill Press, Barrytown, New York 12507, with partial support from the National Endowment for the Arts and the New York State Council on the Arts.

Produced by Open Studio, Rhinebeck, New York, a non-profit facility for writers, artists, and independent publishers supported in part by grants from the National Endowment for the Arts and the New York State Council on the Arts.

Library of Congress Cataloging in Publication Data

Corman, Cid.
    Aegis, selected poems 1970-1980.

PS3553.065A62 1983   811'.54   82-16923
ISBN 0-930794-57-5 (cloth)
ISBN 0-930794-58-3 (paper)

Manufactured in the United States of America.

for Basil Bunting

*After the event
we know. Beyond the
dark fringe of the near*

*hill the crown beyond
of another height
given to sunlight.*

AEGIS

I

Tettix

Our blessing
your — drunk on
dew — from tree
top — royal
lyric. Yours
all the fields
and woods — guest
and host — most
harmless friend
of ours. You
state summer.
The Muses
love you and
Phoebus who
provided
the sound. Age-
less and e-
phemeral —
sage — earthborn —
bound to song.
Feelingless —
bloodless husk —
you might well
be a god.

Bright seaweed reaping
Minume in our passing
the summer grass of
Noshima Head appearing
as the boat comes closer in.

Though you say you'll come
more often than not you don't —
since you say and don't
I won't expect you to come
unless you say that you won't.

May the newest new
year of the beginning of
the spring just begun
today like the falling snow
the more heap up our blessings.

If he could tell me
what he meant beyond
noyse of syllables

In the beginning
where beginning and
end coincide *in*

Then confidently
might I say: True. And
the book be opened.

Touring the world
tilling a small field
to its limits.

High my spirit strove, but love
  Drew it back; pain bent it more;
  So do I pass now through life's
  Arc to whence I once arose.

Morning used to be beautiful
and night fall drew cries — but now
when the day breaks the heart shakes
and the darkness coming compels.

Don't laugh! I made a poem.
You be my one listener.
Craving for community.

Not only to live but to
have something to live for. A
meaning. Otherwise destroy

destroy. Miracle, mystery,
authority. Only outs.
Freedom's individual

a mockery. Belief is
doubt and doubt belief. Thank you.
It's time we were both going.

The Fieldfare

Nothing I have seen
or if — unknown. He —
remembering — saw

one deep winter's day
his father idly
toss a stone at one

half-frozen in the
garden and knock it
dead. The weight the child

then retrieved haunts him
eighty years later:
plumage of a bone.

The Sense

I am the future,
dream of making it
speak. Art capable

of an energy
to this end not yet
fully demanded

of it. And with a
less awkward approach,
a wooing less shy,

an embrace less weak,
it would be able
to draw the foregone

closer to its breast.
What he wanted was
the very smell of

that simpler mixture
that had so long served,
he wanted the tick

of the old stopped clocks,
wanted the hour
this and that happened,

the temperature,
the weather, the sound,
and more the stillness,

the exact look-out,
and corresponding
look-in, through windows,

the slant on the walls
of the light of an
afternoon had been.

He wanted the un-
imaginable,
wanted evidence

of a sort for which
there never had been
documents enough,

for which documents,
though multiplied, would
never *be* enough.

14

The artist's method —
to try for an ell
in order to get

an inch. In such a
case the difficult,
as at best it is,

becomes so dire that
to face it with hope
one has to propose

the impossible.
To bear back the lost
is at all events

much like entering
the enemy's lines
to plead for one's dead

for burial — poor
Priam; and to that
extent was he not

by his deepening
penetration,con-
temporaneous

15

and present? "Present" —
a word used by him
meaning — for most things —

"markedly absent".
It was up to the
old ghosts to take him

for one of themselves —
not a soothsayer
or prophet, much less

a charlatan, with
no claim to the gift
of second sight — but

to confess to have
cultivated the
imagination —

as one has to in
a country where there's
nothing to take that

trouble off one's hands.
Kept on and on by
force of the stillness.

Winterbourne Bishop

I found it
a relief —
a country

with nothing
to draw one
out of town:

wide, empty
nothing to
look at but

a furze-bush —
or from the
summit of

the down — on
a barrow —
the village

cottages
half-hidden
among the

few trees — the
stone tower
of the small

church looking
no taller
than a mile-

stone. And that
emptiness
seemed good: a

relief to
have no thought
of any

thing. But no!
A sense of
elation —

of coming
home: not a
desert but

a place where
men and their
works and their

dwellings are
earthwise un–
obtrusive.

This is the non-existent beast.
They didn't know it but somehow —
its movement, its manner, its throat,
even its quiet eye's gleam — loved.

True, it *wasn't*. But loving it
it became. They always left space.
And in the space, clear, allowed-for,
it lifted its head hardly had

to be. They fed it on no grain,
but only possibility.
And this gave such strength to the beast

it was crowned with horn. One horn.
To a maiden it came, white, near —
and in her mirror was and in her.

So much apple, pear and banana,
huckleberry... All this bespeaks
death and life in the mouth...I sense...
Read it on any child's countenance

as it starts tasting them. This comes from far.
Becomes to you slowly nameless a-mouth?
Where there were only words flow findings
from the fruitflesh surprisingly released.

Dare to say what apple to you states.
That sweetness which first concentrates
to, in the tasting lightly lifted up,

become clear, awake and transparent,
ambiguous, sunny, earthy, present - :
O revealing, feeling, joy —, too much!

Plop of the
fruit fallen,
hymn of the
trees' silence.

Long Night Walk in the Rain at Policoro

Two, two men, of the female element, two boys, two infants, two old men, two ghosts, two ideas of ideas, two fears, two bloods, and one desire, what we were, are, to hang onto, there to be more

here. And we walked, from where we came, back to there, or where we now are, if now is, here, or not ever again together, and never altogether apart, we moved, went. From the house we entered into the house we go out into. Are going. Was

beach. Antiquity. Not that it was the season for the dead, or living, but in-between-times, the clock, hands at halfpastsix, no time at all. And it was dark, or dark when we went out upon it. Went there to get away, to be alone, as if both were not away, not alone, where we were, even before we came. Always as if things, ourselves, were not as we take them, making them. We

ate salt herring drank red wine nibbled stale black bread. Ionian winter. The man lit fire from fresh branches that seethed and crackled and spat flame and our shadows danced back and forth walls and over and over again into deeper darkness. We sat under a sea-lamp and could smell the salt in the grain of the tablecloth and in the wood under it and the wooden beams overhead. The curtains were drawn. We played at fortune, telling. We all wanted to travel, the servingman and ourselves. To go somehow, to go on, and somehow never to lose anything. Yet all the while knowing loss, knowing we had only everything, and nothing, the same,

to lose. We went out into it. And no sea was, only the hushed sound of a buried turbulence, beyond our measure, as if a total light confused with a total dark. I felt myself not even spirit, but the fire within the flame, the light of light, someone else might see by, but to myself and for myself invisible, meaningless for self-meaning. Nothing

seen. I wanted to fall, down, to crumble into earth, but where was down, where was the earth, where was the substance that could fall? I couldn't happen. Never had I felt so lost, so undiscoverable, so irretrievable, and so much beyond ground. And yet I felt, as once when nearly drowned — in the fatal calm — I caught first breath, lights on a distant shore suddenly break

upon me. I all eye at once. And yet not me, but the lights themselves, the further shore, bear me brimming. I feel in the service of darkness. And my friend, who has gone ahead, then speaks, addresses me. The softness of his voice the softness of the rain now begins to fall. I have my cap and let him have my scarf. Arm in arm we hurry on

slowly. The road leads straight from the sea towards home, or where we are staying. And all the homes we pass, the gardens of sand, are locked and dogs bark, fearful of us, trying to share their fear. And

a train crosses our way, but in the distance, a toy carrying a streamer of smoke above it off. And the night sky extends tremendously everywhere. And past the sugar factory, past every ensconced silence, we come striding between the rows of drenched eucalyptus whose green blades flash and a fresh perfume and whose rind the light wind seems to loosen, the huge trees doing the slowest dance. We walk

an avenue. No one greeting us, but everywhere being welcomed, on all sides, and the dogs come forth. And we bark at them and they answer us, know us, excited and quiet. And I think, my friend, O my friends, how I envy us tonight.

27

To be Socrates —
the soldier of snow —
standing there all night

barefoot thinking of
how to resolve night
and then as day breaks

to kneel in the snow —
bow to the rising
replying sun. Know.

Fresh from the bath
with sons and wife
our Socrates

pledging a cock
to the god of
health drinks hemlock.

We savor yet
the fact he could
accommodate.

The Proceeding

"Someone must have"
or why you
here? The question

rests on the plate
a promised
head gazing back

upon a dance
unveiling
the mystery.

Delight in knowing
the name of a thing,
knowing somebody

by reputation.
Things begin to seem,
as they are sounded,

real. Napoleons,
from your asylums
arise. Your madness

meets us as our own.
But you confuse us
insisting that you

alone are you. All
are Christ and Apollo,
the rose and the sun.

These words — this
breath and this —
declare you

Lazarus.
To give you
what you fear —

life again
on the one
term known — death.

Cincinnati

The hatred the
bum greeted me
with — in passing —

each a stranger
to the other —
brings my eyes tears —

for one enough
like me to be
me made him feel

like that. Now years
later I see
I met a friend.

JFK

The nice rotunda
in a direct line
to the obelisk

or does memory
mislead me again?
Anyhow above

the rank and file dead
rightfully, of course,
or what are mountains

to commemorate?
We can speculate
as it pleases us

to do—or what might
have happened if...But
what happened is this.

The Gem

from Wyoming

Morion. The stone
that looks black, made smooth
age after age and

small, as if some smoke
were embedded in
crystal, ash water

Apache tear. As
nearly Arp as Arp
is. Nothing extra.

all edge and no edge.
solid heart. What one
offers another.

The great book
is ended.
We feared it

would end when
we started
and read slow.

Now we think
back to when
we didn't

know what was
to happen
and wish we

never did.
And yet we
never do.

Take my hand —
you say. Though
I know you're

dead. It don't
matter — you
add. As if

you had read
my thought or
shared it once.

And at this
point — beyond
argument —

I reach out —
compelled by
your attempt

to reach me.
Where will you
take me — comes

to mind—but
already
I am led

far beyond
my power
to say where

I am —
        being
wherever
        you are.

Yes, he knew
he would be
the death of
his father,

nothing he
could — in the
face of it —
do, but be

blind — for that's
what wisdom
is. Let me
be your guide.

We are each
each other's,
given to
dying now.

You say God — I say nothing.
What's there to argue about?
Out of need of touch to touch

we came into our own cry.
There are things that are silent.
What can communicate tries.

The point is
not ourselves,
not me — nor —

as it turns
out — you. Then —
we ask — Who?

No who, no
what, no known,
and nothing

to be known.
No point. And
none in this.

And never
the less, this.
Speak to man.

And then you are dead.
You. You want to go
out and touch the edge

of the world — simply
to feel and breathe and
be it and be. Like

he day after day
at Mont St-Victoire
becoming Cézanne.

III

I have come far to have found nothing
or to have found that what was found was
only to be lost, lost finally
in that absence whose trace is silence.

Stuck on the wet track —
melodramatic —
butterfly, yellow
and black. I see it —

on the other side
of the turnstile — strain
to come undone and
know that I could go

and free it. But dont.
Wanting to see it
free itself — I say —
knowing that it wont.

46

I wanted
you to know
Not to say

I love you —
but just for
you to know.

You quote my own words to me
and I think they must be yours —
they are beautiful. Of course,

they *are* yours — as they return
through your affection. I wish
all our words could be so shared.

High Time

For the first time
awakening
and seeing sky

and trees and here
or there a bird
and on the grass —

grass! — dew! And I
am the seeing!
How obvious

it is that I
could never have
imagined this.

Was all this only
to be collected
into the book you

now hold and glance through —
stopping here and there —
as here — caught by a

flicker of meaning —
or is it all my
imagination?

Parabola

*What did you think
I meant?* What does
any of us

mean? The point that
holds between us
a distance we

may move towards
but never reach —
the meanness of

significance
in the face of
actual death.

I want nothing
of the river
and it clearly

wants nothing of
me. Yet as it
flows out of the

mountains into
my eyes the heart
becomes a sea.

I speak but
the figure
in the glass
pretends to

Or is it
its silence
that I mock
in talking.

Uncertain
clouds, the sun —
of course — felt

beyond and
through — as if
the day might

clear. Unclear—
however —
whether this

will occur.
The words lift
from East to

West against
the wind. I
can almost

hear in the
shifting breeze
a friend say —

Corman, who
do you think
you're shittin'?

Ask me when
I am dead
the meaning

of this. Then
each word will
answer you.

The Beggary

Of course, there
is nothing
to say and

what I am
saying is
nothing. But

do you hear
nothing, is
this nothing?

Where would I go
if I could go —
who would I be
if I could be

What would I say
if I had a voice —
and who says this
saying it's me?

And now the
words — remote:
another

life, not this
obvious
makeshift. I . . .?

Dont tell me
who I am
let me guess.

I kneaded the flame
and made of it word.
O eat — eat and make
of the body light.

IV

The Actor enters and takes his seat at center
—facing the audience

I am here. And so are you. We are here, in effect, together. Both are here by choice, though the choice is not quite the same. You presumably came to be diverted and possibly to be made more aware by me, or through me. And I am here presumably because I am an actor and this is my business.

You will notice, perhaps to your chagrin, that I am saying what is only too obvious, but if I were to "act" — and the word is in quotes — you would realize that no matter how stirring the action might be, it would still remain an "act". It is in this sense alone, then, that I am an actor.

The other thing that you will have already noticed — likewise to your chagrin — is that if I keep on saying the obvious, as I am, you are not only likely not to be diverted, but you stand an excellent chance of being bored. And whatever awareness is exerted upon you may be more in the way of an imposition than an elucidation. And in any event you didn't come to be lectured to or edified.

I could, of course, do all manner of things, within the range of the words given me and the director's discretion and my own imagination. The binding situation, however, remains the same: an actor, the actor, myself as it happens, on a stage facing an audience, you as it happens, here.

Is this a "situation"? And if it is, what does it mean to either or both of us (all of us here involved) and in this situation what can I do — what is given me to do — that will completely concern you so that we may mutually benefit from the trouble we have gone to to be together here, or the trouble that was gone to for us—whether wittingly or not — so that we are here together now?

If I go on speaking, even as I do, I might as well, you'll say, be acting out any script for the words I am saying are words that have been provided for me to present to you and, to that extent, I am actor as interpreter. But you are interpreters too and each will read my actions, interpretations of another's ideas, in his own way and may well, in the end, dispute what the show was all about at the end or anywhere along the way. And my being the interpreter — or the author being the author — of the text will by no means mean that any of us can act as authority about what is going on — assuming as we do that something is going on — even if only the act of an actor seated on a stage before a seated, more or less listening, audience, each waiting for something to happen that is either happening or life itself is less than a play.

My acting as an actor apparently is more than analogous to your acting as audience, for the act of listening — and inwardly sharing moment — is a vital conjunct of speaking — even if I were only here alone and speaking to myself. It is, then, reflection in the sense of reflection as thinking. The act of theater becomes an act, mind you an "act", of thinking the common situation through together.

You can say, naturally enough, that the words are given and that is in itself terribly restrictive — but whatever words occur — even at liberty — would be only those words and no others and, in effect, they would be or become the script. The point is, rather, that whatever words occur, whatever "acts", they remain part of a situation that is being shared and how they are being shared, precisely, concerns us.

I don't mean by this that I have come here to tell you how to behave—but havent you come with a rather clear idea of how I, as an actor, should behave and isnt it this "misbehavior" on my part that is more dismaying in the situation to which we are now mutually exposed? I dont know what you will do. As an actor I am supposedly more disciplined, trained, accustomed to, the theatrical (play) situation and, as a result, should be prepared for whatever response might occur to you.

The situation still binds us—so long as you and I let ourselves remain in it, part of it—but it only releases us—and surely this is the crux—insofar as we decisively give ourselves to it.

We might all say that we are awaiting the proper inspiration to really let go. As if, in an older jargon, we waited to be "attuned". Against my words there is the much greater weight of your silence, that silence which we share here as instrument. The instrument, as ancient legend relates to us, will not play at our command, but only out of the lives we have brought to it, the life we confide to it. All we can do is hear it and hearing it find an accompanying song. That song is sometimes realized in silence.

The situation in which we find ourselves is as long as life and as quick as death. The distance that rests between us is less than the speed of light; it is the distance between the lover and the beloved. The language that has been given me to bridge it is—by intention — the language of love, which is faster than light and holds fast life. It does not define life and it does not defy life — or death. It comes of the life that has thought of itself *as* life and finds itself loving it.

It acts only as we have acted, all of us who are here, in being here, by whatever "act" of choice. It is true only as anything is true, as a form of the human imagination that can only confirm that it is by saying it is.

The situation is that we are here to affirm each other as "actors" in a theater, palpably, decisively. And the scene only changes from the indoors of outside to the outside of indoors — as we shift ourselves. Both in and out. Every motion becomes an "act" of love and love itself, if so obvious a matter needs the redundancy of saying, is an "act".

It is not, then, that I am here — centered on a stage — and you are there — at the center of your each universe — but that we revolve around each other, are related

66

and — by being here, by some form of choice — are dearly related . The darkness between us, which might as well be light and will be soon enough, keeps us from seeing perhaps more clearly that we are "home", in a certain place, given to ends beyond our knowing and given, as at this moment, to beginnings of any ends — so that the play does not stop when the lights go up but only then does the "act" open out, enter again the specific world that each of us must enter.

That we have met here and that you have let my words, the words that have been given me to say, come unto you becomes the fullest affirmation of each of us being once at least together. And once is always enough.

The Scissors

Two blades hinged
and closing
edges on

themselves to
cut off this
from this. I'm

instrument —
though — to this
occurrence.

Flower Arrangement

The blind man
feels growing
under his

feet kneels to
reach a grass
to hold it

in the vase
a moment
of his hand.

Trout/Ayu

Whatever it is
what hunger is it
requires it? Wriggling

as the skewer is
thrust through its painful
body. To pick at

the flesh thereafter —
leaving the heart — the
entrails — the bones — on

the beautiful dish.
What ceremony
warrants this dead fish?

In Exasperation

What do you
want of my
young life — our

mother used
to cry to
us children.

We wanted
her — all her
life. Even

now — with her
dead — we want
all her life.

They stand facing each other
hating each other and yet
in their distinctness feeling

how identical they are —
and blinded by their seeing.

They seem to ape each other.

They want to embrace but know
no matter how close they come

they are decisively di-
vided. One is the image,
clearly, of the other. Which?

We look for a way
out of words. How lost
can lost be? Thought will

not eliminate
thought, but learns to play
the game of Yoga.

O animal, man,
be the dying you
you alone contain.

What you are
I am. As if
to admit

the look in the
mirror of
the mirror. Not

nature to
be upheld — but
seen for what

it is: unseen
unless as
an edifice.

The rain re-
lentlessly
effortless

It makes us
look like fools
trying so

hard to be
what we are —
which we are.

It's food. And
if you *are*
hungry,

you know it.
Nevermind
calling

it shit —
shocking us
into sense.

The sense is
this. Come and
get it.

76

It isnt that we
want to die and yet
we do want and want

the death each breath bears
painfully closer
to bear us into

the again binding
rhythm we had — it seemed —
for a time — escaped.

Nothing more
than this. And
this enough.

But no one —
short of death —
admits it.

To reach an
empty
stage

(a
painted
evergreen

for
scenery)
and dance

as only
a ghost
can.

A man says.
Of course. You
know what that

means. You know
what it means
at this point.

To sit in the room
without a light and
feel the evening come

over the garden
into the house. To
feel it coming home.

V

In the flood's
confusion
the shadow
of a bridge.

To embrace
a tree — how
silly can
one get — yet

To want to
dance with it
the way the
wind's doing.

The old pines
axed. Lumber.
And some stumps.

More space at
the temple
now. But roots

alone are
meaningless —
buried mouths.

Pointing out
each rain drop
in the field
the sun light

remembers
all is just
the smallest
part of all.

Work work! Yeah —
it's ok —
crow — for you

to squawk — o-
ver the hill
already.

A cricket
in the field
listening

to itself —
to its self?
Listening?

Somebody!
Somebody
comes

But sometimes
nothing
happens.

A bell selling
money for rags —
or how the world
gets rich.

The rain comes
and the rain
goes. It seems

familiar.
Like something
we might know.

The tide
goes out
and

leaves the
island
land.

.

Resting on
the earth and
gazing at

the heavens —
an infant
at a breast

No one is content —
for every breath
a breath is wanted.

You arrive
just as I
have gone. This

intersects.
The point of
our absence.

To say much and
not to have said
the little meant

A burnt match points
from the ashtray's
edge to the ash.

Follow
the stream:
Dont go —
but be
going.

What is life
a man asks

Only a
man replies.

CID CORMAN

Typeset, designed, and produced by Open Studio, Rhinebeck, New York. Cover design by Susan Quasha. The text type is LSE Bembo; the cover type is Westminster Light. This is an edition of 1500 paper and 200 cloth, of which 43 of the cloth have been numbered and signed by the author.